Your Lone Journey

Your Lone Journey

Paintings by M. B. Goffstein
for a song by Rosa Lee and Doc Watson

Harper & Row, Publishers

Your Lone Journey
Words and music by Rosa Lee Watson and
Arthel "Doc" Watson, © 1969, Hillgreen Music (BMI)
Illustrations copyright © 1986 by M. B. Goffstein
Printed in the U.S.A. All rights reserved.

Library of Congress Cataloging in Publication Data
Goffstein, M. B.
Your lone journey.

1. Goffstein, M. B.   2. Death in art.   3. Death—
Meditations.   I. Watson, Rosa Lee.   II. Watson, Doc.
III. Title.
NC139.G54A4 1986   741.973   86-45107
ISBN 0-06-015659-7

Designed by Constance Fogler
1 2 3 4 5 6 7 8 9 10
First Edition

Your Lone Journey

God's given us years
of happiness here.

Now we must part.

And as the angels come
and call for you,

the pains of grief
tug at my heart.

Oh, my darling!

My darling!

My heart breaks
as you take

your lone journey.

Oh, the days will be empty,

the nights so long,
without you, my love.

And as God calls for you
I'm left alone.

But we will meet
in Heaven above.

Oh, my darling!

My darling!

My heart breaks
as you take

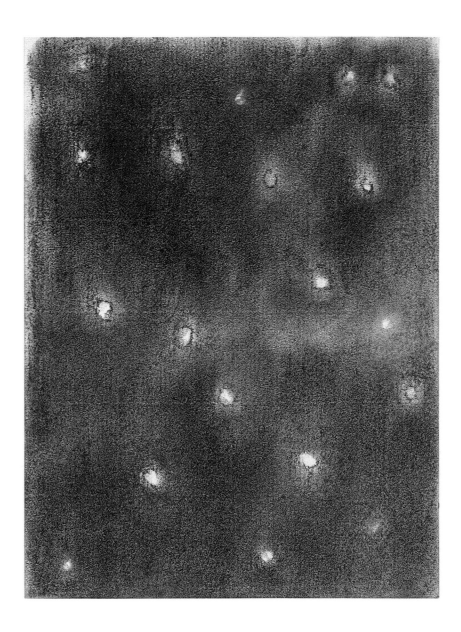

your lone journey.

Fond memories I'll keep

of happy days
that on earth we trod.

And when I come,
we will walk hand in hand

as one in Heaven,
in the family of God.

Oh, my darling!

My darling!

My heart breaks
as you take

your lone journey.